Mourning Dew

Lucy Strange

BookLeaf Publishing

India | USA | UK

Presentation by *BookLeaf Publishing*

Web: www.bookleafpub.com

E-mail: info@bookleafpub.com

ISBN: 9789357747936

First edition 2023

To Violet, the years leading to you have been beyond comprehension. I am so grateful you sprouted when you did. Our family is complete. Love Always, Luce

ACKNOWLEDGEMENT

Thank you Mom and Mamaw, for never giving up. The unconditional support we have for each other has been my driving force for as long as I can remember.

To Jaiden, I adore you always and am immensely grateful for the five-leaf clover I found.

PREFACE

The perfect storm that unleashed years of torment. A story of love, pain, child abuse, sexual assault, addiction, rebirth, resiliency, and courage.

Reality

We come, we go, we rest, we go. Again. Again.
Again.
There's only continuous emergency.
What constitutes as a reason for rest?
There's no right answer, humanity is gone.

My Hero

Off. Nothing. Void.
longing to feel anything
unclear. unknown. unintentional.
waste of space/person of the year
I love you always

Aurora

terror. depression. unworthy. unlovable.
unforgivable.
months pass as the infection spreads
taking root in my soil
When will this sun-drop be too bright to hide
with a basket
thoughts alone won't do it
Aphelia
Allow the meteor to burn solo. Again.
NO. NOT THIS TIME.

Caged

Hello, Goodbye, Nice to see you
until we meet again
for now, we'll have lunch on the moon
play on the rings of Saturn
and wait for when you can hold me again

Violet Flowers

The time for celebration has come
amidst the acid rain
Spring has Sprung

Bluebirds

Passion. Emotion. Love.
our root systems have intertwined
beyond disentanglement
my muse. my mirror.
the drug of which I will never be sober
the dance. my dance.

Boundaries

Tiptoe the choreography
Slow to vocalize
slow to anger
listen as if lives depend on it
Fight for justice regardless of the cost
Be true. Be honest.
Be humble. Be you.

Unconditional

To apologize, to mean it
To change behavior
because someone means enough to you
mistakes chain to you
the weight is overbearing
cut the line
Love is present
There is rest in release
There is unity in forgiveness

Awoken

Joy. Peace. Calm.
everything that's good
pure. lovely. beauty.
at once it made sense
the nightmare is subconscious

Coronation

Kindness. Solidarity. Grace.
the head on your shoulders
means more than aimless bullets
stand strong. keep going.
you were made
for such a time as this

Like Watching Plants Grow

Growth
Stages are unnoticed
Effort gone unacknowledged
Aim for success
attempt. attempt. attempt. attempt.
success. finally success.
The news seeps in like a sponge
absorbing all surrounding molecules
At once you are ready
it is beyond clear
Flower has bloomed

Too Far In To Turn Around

You have jumped
Your nervous system has adjusted
Amidst the chaos
you have clear thinking
panic surrounds you
somehow unfazed
You have learned to fly

Not That Cool

Patience. 2 syllables
1 word. 10,000 implications.
Patience. Things will get better.
just sit still
quiet your voice
don't look
the nightmares come
dominos fall as accidents
are set into future gameplay
If you must glance
the forests burn
questions stir the pride
A family in silence

Perspective

A single spark engulfs
every mal-intended claim
reactants are combined in the beaker
there is no more kinetic energy to exert
although energy cannot be created
or destroyed
transfers occur in every atom
the equation is irreversible
you are left with something
foreign
you decide its value

Hearing The First Cry

Labor is over
your baby draped
over your chest
you feel exhausted
more so you feel
immense amazement
life is new

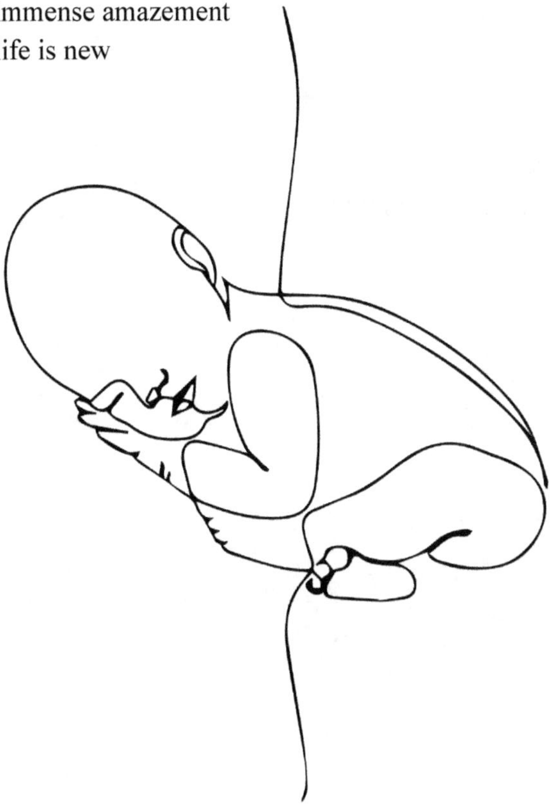

I AM YOURS

How did my body do this
why me to be blessed so big
how do I...
questions flood my prefrontal cortex
no limit to their infinity
"Look at Me"
with this sound
neurons hush in obedience
like a system
finally
reaching equilibrium

Sonrise

Comfort. Warmth. Safety. Care. Appreciation.
I found myself in the water
taken in and made whole
love not used as an excuse
instead used as the
double-edged sword it is
My cup was gifted to me
and expressed full expenses paid
the gate was left open
IAM not alone
I was built on the solid foundation
IAM truly free

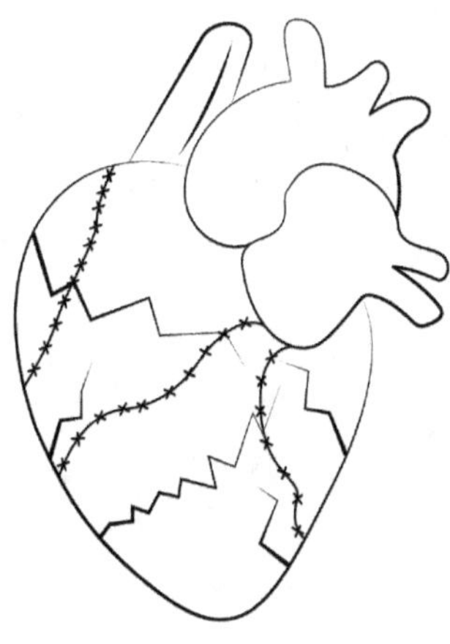

Checkmate

You're too far in to turn around
this chess game
only one-fifth of the way complete
the enemy hisses and spits
waiting for retaliation
the crowd awaits
all eyes on you.
Your-
beliefs. morals. values. fate.
Doubtfulness burns their skin
spreading like a bacterial infection
oozing at the puss-filled sores
You hear the words of the Coach
"Mindfulness. Humility. Grace. Strength."
the vulgarity becomes meaningless
you have returned to the discussion group
this is the same as practiced

I Was Born In Wildflowers

The wind brushes my hair
grass washing my feet
mud moisturizing my skin
sun teaching me compassion
rain pollinating my mind
birds becoming family
animals stay loyal friends
I learn equilibrium from watching
the moon come and go
never dulling
regardless
how much show

Escaping Coil Traps

Children play. Adults raise.
when the vixen is trapped
deep in the woods
lured there by genomes
the kits see unmet needs
within the skulk
we won't submit any longer
our courage, sharpened
our strategy, adaptable
our character, resilient
together we will build the map
hunting for the miracle to save
all who were
all who are
all who will be

Strange

Pinky promises
soft kisses
kind enough to honor
grit enough to last
the children awoke to realize
home has been and always will be